D1154127

THE CHERRY MINDER

THE CHERRY MINDER

FRANK KENDON

LONDON: J. M. DENT & SONS LTD.

MGe

TO
ADAM'S MOTHER

CONTENTS

Man 's an apprentice, and sorrow 's his master.

The Ends of Eden

(But now they desire a better country, that is, an heavenly.)

'OH, when will peace in heaven's full light arise?'
    Lost in the fields, and troubled, Adam lies.
Moon-tempted, darkness every way his prison.
The moon and many stars to mislead his eyes;
And since they rose, uncertain trees have risen,
Dark forms alive, from whose high branches falls
    Music of secret meaning:
'Oh, when will peace in day's full truth arise?
Did not God visit Eden in the evening?'

'Dear wilderness forsaken, was it true?
He came in silence then; by this we knew
His coming, by the sleeping of the wind,
The hanging down of leaves, the fall of dew;
More by distillèd sweetness, filling mind
And body, while the sun stooped low, and sent
    To search the deeps and bowers,
Where now God walks alone.   Can this be true,
Or is it but a fantasy of ours?'

'Eve, Eve,' the darkness said.   And Eve came near,
Heavy with unborn Cain.   She listened there,
While Adam from the grass-of-trouble spoke:
'Tell me I do not dream,' he said, 'Eve dear.'

I

She answered: 'Once 'twas true, but I who broke
God's law so easily, drew an exile on us;
    If Eden be now forbidden,
Earth is our home.   We shall not find him here
Who was our sweetness and bright rest in Eden.'

Then both were silent, that their thoughts alone
Might be companions until morning shone.
'Rose not the sun like this in easts of old?
I see the mists among the cedars blown;
O Eve, the sloping lawns all gold, and gold
The tops of trees that stand above the mists—
    Islands in inland seas.
Surely we are forgiven!   What have we done?
Behold the lawns, the mists, the cedar trees.'

'No, there is nothing changed,' said weary Eve.
'Would heaven there were,' she thought.   'We should
    not grieve
So secretly, perhaps, if all were lost;
Nothing is changed of all that we perceive——'
Just then high up two beating wild swans crossed,
A wren sat singing in the underwood,
    And a stag stepped forth to grass;
As though to make it easier to believe
That Earth was Eden still—for so it was.

Knowledge of death was all that brought their sighs;
Living was still sweet.   But when pleasure dies
A man must contrive some end for life to advance,
And, spending time, must value what time buys.
'We have only strayed,' said he, 'by some mischance.
But you are tired.   Rest here; and I 'll go forth
    To look for our old hill.'
She shook her head; she could not think him wise.
'But let him go,' she thought, 'if go he will!'

So went Adam, down through the grey grass,
And the stag that saw him coming let him pass
With scarcely a nod from his proud, antlered head.
Eve watched him also, smiling, where she was
Among the shadows that the hill trees spread.
At length he turned towards the sun, and climbing,
    Went out of sight.   Straight fell
A dream of solitude.   Dark in the grass
She saw his foot-track through the empty dell.

Wood folded over wood, hill beyond hill,
Where well she knew no footstep ever fell.
Adam had turned and left the world alone,
Eager to catch the irretrievable.
Eve leaned to touch a dandelion crown.

3

Warm to the hand it felt, and her finger shook it,
    Sailing the feathered seeds.
She closed her wakeful eyes, and lay quite still;
The trees of earth bent down their guardian heads.

Bright morning swam above her hollow home;
She drowned in the eddies of a swingeing gloom
Beneath an ancient oak, whose branches rode
Heavily on the surging airs; and a foam
Of golden light upon his branch tips showed.
Soon to the noise of moving leaves she fell
    Soundly asleep, content;
But Adam, shoulder high in grass and bloom,
Sought Eden lost, bewailing their banishment.

Small startled birds and creatures rustled in;
Wild roses shook their dews upon his skin;
Snake slid away between the leaves, without
Stirring a whisper—such had surely been
The life of Eden too!   O cunning doubt,
Born of sound reason.   Yet not this their dwelling,
    This shaken peace not theirs.
Abroad, how like the garden; how, within,
Solemnly changed, and charged with sudden tears.

4

He crept through thickets.   Every rising mound
He clambered up.   In vain he stared around:
All seemed and was not Eden, old was new
To his quick eyes.   Often he thought he found
Fragments of Eden, paths that wandered through
Familiar orchards into strange, wide valleys;
      He ran to touch the bark
Of some remembered fruit tree, but still found
In likeness difference, still in light some dark.

Eve slept and woke.   Her husband struggled on.
A ring-dove made a spirit of the noon,
Calling him up, out of the silent plains,
To stand and dream of God, as Eve had done
Sometimes, unwittingly.   He climbed with pains
Of body and soul, and on the murmur heard
      His own hard breath.   Then spoke
To the empty air, first human sorrow known
In those long whispering vaults of waiting oak.

'Wherefore to feed on beauty didst thou teach
My dying spirit, giving sense and speech
To friable clay, but stealing hope away?
What love is this beyond our highest reach
That we can apprehend, but not obey?

Hidest thou, God of Heaven, behind thy promise,
    Or art thou in this place?
I know thou art here unseen, though I beseech
The twilight vainly, and the emptiness.

'What virtue is in dying, God to ordain it?
If life must end, why trouble to sustain it?
What matters fruit be sweet, if no one taste it,
Or Eden dear, if we may never regain it?
Little our love or mighty, all is wasted!
Had Eden never been, had we not lived
    So to defile thy glory,
Thou hadst a heaven of angels to maintain it;
It needed not our sick and empty story!

'Show me some reason, Lord, before I die,
Why all this living beauty with the eye
Must perish; why the thoughts of days dissolved—
Far better than the moment going by—
Must be with me in vile terror involved.
Or why must either Eve be left lonely,
    Losing me, whom she loves,
Or I live on, and she be memory,
Without a throat to laugh with? O long groves,
6

'And shadowy lawns, and flowers of Eden's grass,
Who sees you now ?   What reckless lovers pass
From shade to shadow, feeding every sense ?
Is empty Eden paradise that was ?
Blooms the sweetbrier so well since Eve came thence ?
No, no!   Bereft of us, who could enjoy you,
    Unhappy you must lie;
And the birds in your lost branches cry: *Alas!*
Adam and Eve, Adam and Eve must die.'

Deeper in gloom he trod, and deeper too
His heart fell into dark, till midday's blue
In open heaven was thickly blotted out.
Suddenly under the boughs a great wind blew,
Sighing more heavily than Adam's doubt:
This died through whispering and melancholy
    To silence deep and close,
Till not a leaf fluttered the forest through,
Far sang no bird, near rustled not a mouse.

Fear smote him from the living quietness;
He touched a tree to solace his distress,
Having no other friend alive to aid him;
Eve was far off, and Eden a lost place,
And God hidden or angry, having made him.

Or was it death's accession, this cold stillness—
　　To speak with Eve no more,
Passive to stand so, watching beauty's face,
Body and soul in loud and fruitless war?

A sunny circle flittered on his hand
Where brown upon the tree it lay, first tanned
By the gold days of innocence.　He stirred—
And full upon the stretched ear of the land
Fell the clear flute notes of one lonely bird,
Shining through silence, as a star through midnight,
　　Echoing, every note,
So that the heart of Adam, and the land
Of trees about him, lived in that bird's throat.

To hear, he sank upon the ferns and wept.
Noon turned to afternoon, and Adam slept,
Worn out with watching night and following day.
His sleep was long; for when he awoke, except
For summer lightnings faint and far away,
And a green glitter where the moon looked under,
　　Thick dark the forests were.
He climbed the difficult hill perplexed, and stepped
Into the grey and moon-enchanted air.

Cold, silver night-mists touched him on the lips,
Brown hung the moon above the bramble tips,
Softly far down a little owl cried low:
'Eve, Eve,' it shouted out of the tangled deeps,
Stealing the thoughts of Adam.   Even so
Called Adam through the fresh and scented air,
      Softly, for darkness' sake.
No answer!   Then said he: 'Far west she sleeps,
And owl and I are all on earth that wake.'

Follow him down!   He hears what follows him,
And thinks 'tis bushes closing.   Let him dream!
He dimly knows again the morning's road,
Till fogs beset him.   Then, as one might swim
Under deep cloudy water, Adam strode
Through the drenched herbage, blind, himself his world,
      Calling for company.
He still thought Eve was far away from him;
But she was near, and answered suddenly:

'Stay there, and talk to me out of the mist.'
'Let me come nearer, Eve; in sight at least.'
'Please wait,' said she.   'Have you found Eden yet?'
'Almost,' said he, remembering his quest;
'I have no news, but that the leaves are wet,

That earth is wide and wild and full of silence.
    But I shall seek again.'
Eve's firstborn cried a little at her breast.
'It is our son,' she said, and brought him Cain.

          *   *   *

Eve never sought, and Adam never found,
For all his sighs, that consecrated ground.
But in deep silence, and in tempests wild
There walked on earth a more than earthly sound,
So that earth seemed an Eden to the child:
Who grew to love, like Eve, a thousand flowers;
    Until of death she taught him.
Then Cain perceived that God was in the sound,
And far and wide, through hope and doubt, they sought
    him.

They found him weeping by the riverside.
'A curse on God and life!' he bitterly cried.
'Is all this nothing that you said was fair?'
Eve tried to comfort him, and Adam tried.
'Living is sweet, my son.' 'Too sweet!' he sware,
'A mockery of sweetness! I 'll defy it;
    Death shall serve my hand!'
Abel was dying at his altar's side,
And Cain an outcast in a haunted land.

NOW she stands high in beauty,
   Now she sinks low in pride,
Arise, my strength, and fight for her!
   My heart arose, and died.

Tall foxgloves on the wind's touch
   Bowed as I went by,
I marked them less than blind men,
   For love was in my eye;

And field roses and rich trees
   And grass, leaves and all,
I swore it was but desert,
   For fire was in my soul.

Here in the stony darkness,
   I find the street in flower,
I make my prison a garden,
   And smell the sudden shower,

And catch my breath for summer
   Full on a southern down,
Here in the stony darkness
   Of this love-lighted town.

To-morrow I will triumph,
    And set my lips on truth;
Leave me my lies to-night,
    And the wild hopes of youth.

'Now stands she high in beauty,'
    A thousand such have cried.
Leave dumb until to-morrow
    'Now sinks she low in pride.'

East Cliff

DROWNED at my foot she lay,
  Her hair fell over the grass;
I could not think, I would not pray,
  So still in strength she was.

Like ivory were her hands;
  She saw, and passively
She let them rest upon the strands
  Of grass, like ivory.

Now for an hour beat not
  The heart the world that tried;
The never-ending battles of thought
  And passion died.

The wind crept through the turf
  Above the precipice;
A linnet near, and the sunken surf,
  Sang, and sang this:

'The hour that flies, in flying
  Lessens not its worth—
Here at your foot, content, is lying
  Daughter of heaven and earth.

13

'Keep still, and be like her,
    Time's master, not his fool——'
I saw the remotest seas astir.
    Deep under, in a pool

Bluer than heaven even,
    In waves the water crept;
And shadows of clouds born in heaven
    Lay on the sea and slept.

The Cry

I CAN see beauty spire and spring
  From mud, or leap like trembling flame
Swiftly into the sorrowing air,
  And die again, as though in shame;

I can see flower-cups at noon
  Beaten to ground by wasting hail,
And hedges of hot roses shake
  Their colours down before a gale;

I have seen sculpture made in flesh,
  Hands that I loved carved still by Death,
And did not shrink from bitter thought,
  Laying to love's foot my cold wreath.

Why then, why did this heart cry out?
  Foreseeing all, it should not cry.
All that we love is doomed and must
  Give way to nature, all must die.

If hopeless strong irrational love
  Could look these death's examples down,
Why at the very wounding stroke
  Have I cried out?   I must have known.

So deep is Death

SO deep is death in silence lapped,
   So deep in sleep their spirits are
Who, out of tempest earth escaped,
   Lie down untroubled.   Like a star
On the rich beds of evening skies
   Before the night has peopled heaven,
So deeply shut from love she lies,
   And her quick going is forgiven.

Come little Spring, come, give us heart;
   Come noisy Summer, sing and drowse;
If sense must now play double part,
   Come life again!   She will not rouse;
She will not hear, nor laugh to hear,
   Whatever challenge wildness make;
Music is silence in her ear;
   Only her lovers lie awake.

Do you hear ?

DO you hear that sighing
    Like the fall of the sea ?
It is only the soft wind
    Singing to the tree.

Do you hear cocks crowing,
    A far-stretching pride,
Answering each other now
    From side to hill side ?

And the shrill repetition
    Of a jenny wren's song,
Spun from the quickset
    That will leaf before long ?

Do you see the bright edge
    Of a leisurely cloud
That swims under the sun
    Because he was proud ?

Did you feel the cold rush
    Of his shadow's wing,
Darkening for a time
    To winter our spring ?

Such things, to receive you,
   I would drive from my head.
To-day as I saw them
   I forgot you were dead.

Now you are in your Country

NOW you are in your country,
 And I, locked fast in mine,
Walk the white roads in silence,
 And see my sun decline.

I see the whole west breaking
 In flame again, to-night;
And earth to peace receding
 Through valleys of delight.

Sleep, in your pleasant country,
 Lie down at last, content,
The hills of constant heaven
 Your dream's bright battlement;

Know that the stars you talk with
 Have eyes on fields at home,
Or buds on banks you dream of
 Now break in scented foam;

For death has hung no silence,
 Nor spring withheld one sign,
Since you turned to your country
 And left me locked in mine.

Resurrection

DRY bones shall rise and live;
  From the deep mines of fire
Streams of hot gold shall give
  New strength and old desire.

Then in the valleys where
  Lost in time they lay
To war shall they prepare,
  And harness Night and Day.

The Flesh that they put on,
  The Blood to fill their veins,
With labour must be won
  And terror, and bitter pains;

But when the battle joy
  Sets their steel nerves in tune,
When, living to destroy,
  They call on sun and moon

To help their sensual eyes,
  Then in the strength of hate
They will not heed the cries
  Of suffering flesh, but wait!

20

Then will gods arm in haste;
　　Then star will shout to star
Across the ethereal waste,
　　Warning the gods to war.

Arm!　Arm!　Creation arms!
　　The maker fears the made!
And a noise of mad alarms,
　　Of heavenly cannonade,

Goes sounding down through space
　　To strike the fearful dumb . . .
But from death's hiding-place
　　The rebel ranks shall come.

Reluctant Sorrow

I SCORN no palaces,
  Nor overpass cottages;
All doors are on latch for me;
  I am a silent new-comer.

Dear lovers fear when
  By a strange echo comes
A bird through their brain
  Bound on a star-journey.

Pole to pole, roads are mine
  To come by, to tread upon;
Lightly I shall come
  And lightly leave in time.

Bear with me in my need;
  Grudge not the hearth-seat.
When I come softly in
  With modest eye, forgive it.

Time was never yet
  That I could be slighted.
I am the mother of
  Quiet and a calm heart.

If you should bar the door,
   Your heart would break and die;
I must come in and stay;
   But none knows my going, ever.

Sudden Encounter

I ROSE from my lamplighted books,
      And went outside to darkness for an apple;
There I saw the new moon in the west,
Like a golden sickle.
The dog whined softly, so I turned aside
To set him free.
I heard an acorn tumble,
And wind in the tree.
Shutting the door of the apple-loft again,
I stared in silence idly at the moon,
A moment in a multitude of years.
My hand was at the latch of time unknown:
There, in delight I knew, but not how keen,
All my youth had quietly come again,
And quietly gone.

WHAT 's this head ? you ask me.   This
     Is the fruit of idleness.
I was tired of words, and she
Came to call, to call on me;
I was tired of custom too,
This unknown came breaking through—
Custom, labour, poverty
Fled when Rachel called on me.

Nine she was.   Nine long years
And still she held that earth was hers;
'Why,' said she, 'your fire 's so small
It must burn very little coal.'

One night in an idle barren mood
I took a piece of polished wood,
And, scarcely thinking, said I saw
A face there, and began to draw.
For lack of better things to do
I drew it and engraved it too,
Till, angry with my mindless tools,
I threw the thing to help my coals.

Next day, with sleep refreshed, I found
This proof-in-process on the ground—
The block was burnt, but this was saved;
This head, unfinished, ill-engraved,

What spirit, stronger than my mind,
Had steered my fingers ?   I was blind—
I did not know, I had no skill,
No patience to go on, no will,
But the mere wish to keep awake;
How could my hands unguided make
This little head, which plainly showed
The look of Rachel, cut in wood!

Appeal

I SPOKE not, I listened not, I loved not, I laboured not,
  Awaiting the turn of season I was content,
Not as dull clay or heavy pyrites
Or rock, but as water in a peak-borne tarn.
Then a round bud, on which my idle eye
Rested in jeopardy of peace, unbudded:
Green flakes unfolding from the shut corolla
And the gold petals silently bestirring.
  It swelled to the air like flame in a cave,
Cupped itself under the sun, and moving
Swayed on the wings of its life,
To a measure of delight.
  Then I felt pleasure
In the gold-dusted cavity,
Molten, endowed with a time-scorning patience,
And hope as immortal as the sun.
  O break upon my fast-budded frozen faith,
Give glory again and the flame of astonishment,
Listen while I speak, or speak if I listen!
My hands ache for work, my life to be stirring,
Call me—let this be beginning, and my answer
Ring in its willingness loudly melodic,
Keen-edged, flame-tongued, fruitful, golden.

On my way Home

ON my way home, the day before yesterday,
    I met Apollo, on his way home.
He knew that I saw him, and nodded to me pleasantly
Out of his meditations, where I could not come.

Ever since then, through sleep and through business,
The buried boy in me is heartlessly living;
I have heard ewes call to their lambs again
Across the lost pastures, through the rainy evening.

Broken-hearted with joy, crying with it, tearless,
My chained spirit hurts a little, dimly and dumb.
Foolish things, bubble words, arise in irrelevance,
They smell of spring rain that fell twenty years ago.

Dance, disobedients!   The prison key is lost which
Should out with you, daringly; the ripe time is fled.
I am old in impotence; quite deaf, I tell you;
Rain never falls, and the fattened flocks are dead.

Christmas Past

WINTER could work no pain that night.
　　The frost was white, and cold was keen;
On black boughs hanging the Bear was bright—
(Stars in leaf-time are seldom seen.)
Still with music, an empty air,
Breathing where the grass grew most,
Sang to a shepherd waiting there.
　In the silence he heard a host
Of voices while the moon began,
Redder than the sun retiring—
Oh, sweet heavens!　That cold man—
His ear engrossed in angel-quiring—
I was that shepherd!

GO into the sun.
    Do not search and question it . . .
In the black vaults
Green Death doubts himself!
   Crimson in the summer
The mad flowers toss,
And tress upon tress
The light trees breathe of it,
And with a million mouths
The growing grass drinks of it.
   Fast underground
In an echo argument
Thou and Thyself
Come to no answer.
(Cold and moss-incrusted
Thy mind's charnel finger-bones;
Thy lungs' chill intake
And moist exhalation
Roars in thy ears.)
   I am a green light in a far place!
Dear corridor prisoner, I am a reed's rustle—
The fall of a rose-leaf—
The smell of a sunburnt hive!

Idleness

('To begin with us on Monday week.')

O THOU sweet Idleness,
    I must not love or listen;
Cover up thy quiet face,
Sing not, ask me not;
By the strings of my heart
I am bound, and would break them;
Take away thy hands.
We must hereupon part.

Come then, embrace:
One empty farewell!
Oh, leave me the grace
To break thy last spell,
For I go, as I dare not,
Hating, though I must,
To fight where I care not,
And be paid in dust.

Obedience

SHE sang!   Sweet was the sound
    Above the subdued roar of the city, clean
Crystal, lifting and refreshing the heart—

From a bright sky, from a god's hand,
A stone dropped into the mantled water;
Back drove the green idleness far,
And the water leapt, waveletted.

Like thick coils of smoke the sound
Of the heaviness of labour twisted,
Involving the brittle shell above,
Clouding the bright silence with foggy roar.

She spoke!   Sweet was the sound,
Above the subdued roar of the city, clean
Crystal, lifting and refreshing the heart.

City Spring

A POWDER of green on the ebony trees;
  A wilder fluting above the drums;
Thoughts upon wind, and embassies
Out of Arcadia, entering slums
And alleys and echoing causeys, where
The day dries winter out of the stones—
This poignant secret stings in the air,
Aching a million hearts at once.

Clear without call—a ten-mile leap
To a cleaner green, to cowslip scent,
To moving heavens by streams as deep
As clouds' reflections. It killed content,
Unbalanced with joy the workaday mood,
Robbed the tills of banks by dreams—
Bursting the buds of varnished wood,
Flecking with foam unvisited streams.

The Echo

THE dogs had run away in lambing time,
  My sister's dog and mine; and she and I,
Fearing the farmer's anger (though the crime
Of racing sheep was not in our dogs' manners),
Set out in rainy twilight down the lanes
To call our calls across the fields.
The spring was moving underground,
Though not as yet awake or visible;
A winter tang still lent the watery air
Some cruelty of coldness;
Not water from the wells of spring,
That deep elixir, which the world and we
Would drink together in a week or two;
But February rain in March,
A cold to endure, not coolness to enjoy.
Behind us what was left of day
Silvered the west beyond the hill,
And when we turned, as country dwellers will,
To see where we had come (although we knew
The lane by inches), half the dying light
Shone on the twisted road in ruts and pools.
We called and we called.   In turn we sent our voices
Flying like messengers this way and that
Over the patient meadows, and at last
Day quickly went from us without a sign.

34

'What shall we do?' we asked.   'Shall we turn back?'
'When they are tired of hunting they 'll come home.
They may not be this side at all,' we said;
'Nobody saw them go.'   But while we talked
We did not halt, we leaned into the rain,
And went a little further.   Presently,
Where the road bent at the bottom of a hill,
And, in the greyness, fields of grass rolled up
Towards the ragged sky, we stopped
As if by impulse, and together turned
Away from the high pastures; and the rain
Came down upon our shoulders.   In the west,
Beneath a heavy cloud that filled the sky,
A long white silver gash of light ran low
Among the naked trees along the ridge.
We waited in the valley; listening, heard
The sad rain's rustle, as it fell unseen
On hedge and bank about us,
And the churning hollow noises,
Swirl and cloop of water,
In the overflowing ditches.   Then we called . . .
And at our call the sobbing world was wild with echo
       voices—
Beneath the dripping darkness,
Calling to one another
In faint remote succession,
Dying softly down to silence,

Softly down, to silence. . . .
  For a moment we stood together, driven
To wonder at the populace of fear
Which night kept hidden from us,
And then the roar of the rain returned upon us,
And the halls of the woods we could not see
Were all empty again.

The Cherry Minder

HARK! What was that, that shot? you cry.
  Why, all day long this summer world,
So full of birds and leaves and flowers,
Must thus be shaken, and its peace destroyed,
Split by shots from a hidden gun.
  It is the cherry minder, new at work,
Now returned from his long winter journeys
With nothing but his hunger and a gun:
A man whose beard and hair have grown like weeds,
Because of so much sleeping under hedges;
One whose noise, whose gun and giant shout,
Is known about here like a sign of June.
  I saw a bird alive to-day,
A blackbird with a bill of gold,
And on his bill a red-hot cherry stuck,
Burning bright in the morning light.
I knew he was a thief;
He ran along the lawn in laurel shelter,
Taking food to his great family,
Where they live in the ivy leaves.
Cherries more to-morrow, more and more,
He will cleverly steal and bring,
Till that great brood have taken wing;
Unless the gun, of which he takes the chances,
He and a hundred others, carelessly,

Should once be pointed up through leaves and branches,
Up to the bough where he sits thieving high.
Then with a crack and a sharp hot pain
His life will all be over.
     Yes, but hark!   Behind us all,
Behind the cherry minder, go
Steady footfalls.
Have you not seen, in darkness, once,
A hand stretched out to touch whatever is near—
You, perhaps, or your dear lover,
Or me whom you have hardly heard about,
Or this old cherry minder
With his giant shout—
Haha!   Hoorooah!   Roar!   Ha!   Ha!?

Full Circle

SHE went up, the moon went up,
  Over the river, the heaving shoulder of
Grassy hillock, over the tree-tops,
Above the invisible kingdom of the sea.

So steadily she went that, being watched,
She only stood, and yet in half an hour
Had lost her swarthy look, and driving herself
Among the first stars, blew them out with her light.

  The moon borrowed my eyes that night
'Twas I that blew the clouds away.
I saw trees toss and shake and stagger
Grey over grasses and gaunt black shadows.
Owls filled the night with their own sweet shocks of fear.
Plovers cried, and thought they were lost for ever.
A pasture horse shuddered his nostrils.
The glassy river tinkled and glittered.
Plunge went the fat vole under the lily leaves—

  She went up, the moon went up;
And there lay hills on their shadow sides,
Roads their nerves.
A cottage a spark was; sheep strayed unfolded,

Cropping the wet short grass steadily
With a soft tearing noise all night, unfolded, scattered.
They taste the thyme and the bitter leaves
And the sweet cold strings of the grass.

They cannot sleep night away like a shepherd.
His candle is cold by the bedside Bible,
Blind is his cottage window,
His arm is warm under his wife's head.
To breathe to dream, to breathe to sleep—
Love is quiet and idle in darkness.
The moon is hindered by curtain and blind.

She went up, she reared over her zenith,
She turned her head the other way,
She did not smile nor change her light,
Though the slow shadows swung slowly, slowly
Under the trees and eaves and under
The following hills.
At last she began to stoop inland
Over forests that sea wind never swayed—
Softly down slipping, softly slipping.
And now the golden lion leaps on the rim of the sea,
His roar shatters, his golden throat cries light.
The stars slink in wherever they stand;

The moon is meekened and loses her royalty.
In pastures spots of dew catch fire,
And sheep stop cropping lips and lift their heads.

From his warm dream the shepherd wakes;
He lifts her head from the crook of his arm,
Kissing the eyelids; stoops to kindle
The fire of to-day on a hearth still warm.
To count the fleeces is all his skill.

 . . . . .

The daylight moon rides like a bubble,
The sun like a lion roars up the sky.

The Footbridge

TORN clouds the wind drives lightly
    Across to-day's high blue,
And leaves that budded yesterday
Let golden sun run through;
By the little river
They stand and dip and stand;
In silver strip the river runs
Through empty pasture land.

See, how a bed of brooklime,
As blue as eyes, receives
An air that laughs in idleness
Among its dripping leaves;
And, streaming under water,
Long green cresses toss,
And white bubbles burst themselves
Against the staining moss.

Here, solitude achieving,
The halcyon may be seen,
Flashing against the water-brook
His red and blue and green;
Wasting his bright beauty;
A wild and timid bird,
Gone like a flash at the first step
On wooden footbridge heard.

What is man's coming and going?
These colours ask no eyes.
Before I pass, and afterwards,
How carelessly he flies!
The flowers will take an ancient wind,
The waters curve and shine—
Only the bridge will fall to ruin
For lack of hands like mine.

Autumn Evening

NOW the dewfall evenings come,
Now the robin sings alone,
Now about the labourer's home
Dark begins ere work is done.

Leaves look bright against their death,
Gold disdainers of all doom,
Nor can any man with truth
Censure death beholding them.

Now through mist the morning rises,
Now the fields are grey with down,
Apples rosy with their wine
Lie in heaps by orchard houses.

Now to catch the last of flies
Spiders multiply their nets;
Swallows in young eagerness
Loudly argue longer flights. . . .

Now on wildly parted trees
Leaves go cold and fall away:
Winter sits in dreadful ease,
Waiting for the world's decay.

Battle Song for Spring

BEAT in earth's breast, O Spring!
　　Though life was pain, she was living;
Return, with a lift of the wing,
　　Wheel and wing back, forgiving!

No peace of sense, no sleeping!
　　But come with a flash of swords,
White from the ground up-leaping
　　To battle-calls of the birds.

Shake through the hill-top sky
　　That conquering flare of day,
Till mud and meadow reply
　　With colour and wild array—

Send wind and parching frost
　　And the sun, unbearably bright;
Cry unto earth, she is lost;
　　Mock her with morning and night,

Until, from her stupor scorned,
　　She wakes to a lusty answer,
Laughs, being battle-warned,
　　And runs to this war, a dancer!

A Kingfisher

IN joyful imitation of old wars,
    I shot my new-made arrow into air.
It soared as if alive; as though the bow,
That now stayed slack and sprung in my left hand,
Had given it life and purpose, and I think
Part of me mounted, young and swift again,
Beside the flying arrow.   What remained—
The bow and body—in the finished act
Stood like a nerveless carving, and my joy
(For that 's alive) shot forth with sight, and shared
The arrow's steady, speedy, singing flight.

    On into evening, up, against the wind,
Free of all timely hopes and earth's deflections,
Winged was I with an aim, of which I knew
Nothing but that fair sky.   But oh! before
The sky was nearly attained, I also felt
Earth's growing weight upon the heavy barb,
Drawing away its vital speed, until,
The highest reached, with lovely dropping curve
My arrow turned in air, and fell and fell,
Gathering downward speed again.   And I,
I turned as well, I felt my spirit turn,
Gently and naturally, gathering love,
Until the arrow hurtled past the tops
Of twilight trees, and struck the earth,

And stood quivering there.
  Then, over the intervening meadow crept
The soul to my lost body, and the bow
Lowered in my left hand.   Time is, I see,
A foolish fiction, after all!   Why, even
In those brief tickings of it, arrow and I
Had lived our lives out and come back to earth!
  At last, across the dew, counting my steps,
I went to fetch the arrow, while the sun
Drew down behind the blue edge of to-day:
I had been blessed, I thought, and was his brother:—
It did not much surprise me when (how rare)
A kingfisher flashed over to a branch
Above the pond, to watch me as I passed.

SHALL we still wrangle,
  Struggle and cry?
Oh, why not entangle,
Live life and let die,
Together, espoused,
Body and I?

Come, THOU, without reason,
Profit, or ill:
Without need or season,
Come, without will:
Look up and frown not!
Ah, Love, stand still!

What a wild power
Hast thou over all!
This earth—thy flower!—
Thy nothing-at-all!
This heaven—thy dominion:
This brain thy thrall!

Art thou the Weaver
Whose fingers shall tie
Quiet into fever
Comfortably—
That knot for whose secret
Many men die?

The Candle Lover

WHEN I walked home from my delight
   One winter night—but nearly spring—
And when she could not tell me, quite,
Whether whatever I could bring
Might win the heaven she must withhold;
That winter night, when wind blew cold
On hill-tops where I walked from her,
I saw across the valley shine
A sudden window light, and there,
Clear on the dark, its hope was mine.

I stopped; and like all lovers, hung
My highest hope on one chance gleam;
That window light, so suddenly sprung
Upon the darkness, could but seem
A light from heaven to break my doubt—
But as I watched, it was blown out:
Someone unknown had carelessly
Snatched brightness from me; and as low
In useless dark I sank, to see
That taper's light extinguished so.

At foolish fancy then I smiled:
'People must go to sleep,' said I;
But all the time that watchful child,
My heart, believed its augury.

Pitch dark the natural world remained,
Under the wind the tall hedge strained,
And then, for some unknown desire,
The sleeper could not sleep to-night;
I saw the sudden spurt of fire,
And then the window's peaceable light!

Song

ALL flowers that ever sun revealed
    Run lightly in her mind;
In her the scorch of sun unsealed
Lilies that April cannot yield—
    Nor any other searcher find.

Oh, should her kindness light on me,
    How can my tongue not boast?
Of all the slavish world to be
Outsingled by that very She
    Whom I did fear and honour most!

The Danger

WHETHER to break the dream,
　　And hear her Yes or No,
Or to look and live and seem
　　Indifferent, lest she go?

Whether to bear this, even,
　　For the sake of quick joy,
Or to throw the dice for heaven
　　Or what must heaven destroy?

O Love, I cannot lose
　　The riches of a glance;
I would not have her choose,
　　Yet cannot trust in chance.

Here then, I speak,—Oh, give me
　　Not words, for they will fall,
But her look to receive me
　　For love, or not at all.

Advice to the Wind

THIS tree came out in blossom gay;
    The ruffian wind passed down her way;
There she stood as white as cream,
Laced about with a strait sunbeam;
Poised as proud as innocence, tall,
Under the shelter-boughs of all
The chestnuts, birches, alder, and ash.
    What should a right wind do but dash—
Have her in his arms? But no—
There she shook, light as snow,
Proud as maidenhood, a sword,
Silver-shooting, set in sward,
Or a flame against the hill,
Or a saint whose kiss would kill.

Go! Herd the red and gold and white!
Sail the moon through scuds at night!
Steal the scent of birch in showers,
The primrose promise, the colour of flowers
That need no sweetness, and convey
With spring such homage as might pay
The loss of one creased petal of hers!
Asking nothing, offering much,
Love is yours at the first touch.

Bright was the Morning

BRIGHT was the morning and the day fair,
   High were the clouds that sailed the clean air,
The land was rich and the herbage fine
Under heaven—and the world was mine.

Thirty crops have burdened to breaking
Boughs of trees, and gone to my making;
Ten thousand days, and every one
A grain of gold from a minted sun.

I bring you the dust.   I long ago knew
That it grew for giving away; but you
Hid long in the world I worshipped—came
Like spring upon winter, a thought, a flame.

Oh, burn my pride, that mortal sin,
My fire-sweet lover!   Let us begin
A single search where two were of old,
And find the beginner of all this gold.

To a wild Linnet overlooked

I KNOW this music!   Happiness wildly is
  Born of it, brook-like.   Silence a song is,
Clear unto eyes unenvious.   And deeply do I
Drink the swift motion, the slow outstretching,
The wary pause, this and that way sharply to
Question the green earth out of your bird's bright
Timorous eyes.

Oh, do not fear us; we are not bound by
Any stale laws of hatred, now we are
Travellers, sightseers, lovers, and searchers
Whose nurture is neither death nor exhaustion of
Any sweet life, but vision and sudden
Surprise of the exquisite spirit; the song,
The silence of joy, that, unconscious in you,
Fountains to heaven.   While we saw we rejoiced!
O bird that sat preening, reposing, enjoying
Warm days before spring.

The Wind and the Corn

*T*HE wind across the standing corn,
   Upon an August day :—
When you were green, that now are ripe,
I kissed the Maid of May.
She had hawthorn petal shells
On her cap and gown;
But I came over Grasstop Hill
And blew the petals down.

In thirty days, or thirty-one,
About the first of June,
When you were ankle-deep and dark
Beneath a growing moon,
I stole softly here and there,
Softly far and near;
In river meadow or Grasstop Hill
I could not find my dear.

When you are reaped, that now be ripe,
You will not feel the rain;
But I shall wake with new-year spring
To find the Maid again.

Cherry petal shells she 'll wear
In her morning gown,
And I 'll come over Grasstop Hill
And shake the petals down—
　　Down, down, down again,
　　And shake the petals down!

. . . And ladders leaning against damson trees,
And idle spades beside old garden walls,
And broken sickles covered up in leaves,
And baskets wet with dew, waist deep in grass,
And spider webs across half-open gates . . .

And memory of a moon, a giant rolling,
And, brown in moon's noonday, prolific oaks,
Glint of moonsilver on their solid acorns . . .

And a fierce sun melting the fringed horizon,
Cold grass, hard apples fallen and forgotten,
And dew-logged thistledown . . . And crackling beechmast,
And plump matt mushrooms—beggars' harvest—white
As chalk, bland as a nut, and pink to break . . .

And bonfire incense, and bracken gold as beech,
And bearded hedges, latest blackberries,
Half-ploughed stubble and dusty threshing yards,
And early nights, cloud multitudes on fire . . .
Dry noons, drenched dawns, deep scents, bright stars,
        lost thoughts . . .

And empty orchards and wide open fields,
And robin solos in deserted woods,
And chimney smoke, and starry candlelight,
And far-off fields, and distance like the past,
And mossy silence, and the scent of leisure,
And spider webs across half-open gates,
And broken sickles buried under leaves,
And idle spades beside old garden walls,
And ladders leaning against damson trees, . . .

The Tea Caddy

IN days when Doctor Johnson's weight
　　Of word and substance felled the great;
While Boswell yet was taking notes
On Goldsmith's doubtful taste in coats;
When all the reverend dead he met
Were living and not reverend yet;
When names had bodies, which sat down;
When Cowper scorched his dressing-gown;
When Blake went hungry down at Felpham,
Or Hayley's hand was moved to help him;
When kings, known only now by statue,
Out of red eyes looked really at you;
When men wore wigs as a matter of course,
And the only travellers went by horse,
And streets were dark and quite unfit;
When a man with brains was called a wit;
When thieves were hanged for being thieves;
When trees in spring put forth green leaves;
When summers were dry or wet or hot,
Or whatever the summers before were not:
In those far days of ill and good
A certain workman chose the wood,
Sharpened tools and set them true,
And worked to make this box for you.

No gaslight ever lit his shop;
He had no wheels to start and stop;
No hot, metallic engines there
Disturbed the shaving-scented air;
His hands were engines, and his eye
His gauge to measure beauty by.
Each box he made remained itself—
He had no copies on his shelf;
And though he made a thousand, this
Is not like any other piece.
How gently time went by for him
Up in that workshop! which grew dim
At sunset time: and then he 'd lay
His chisels down, and sweep away
The chips and shavings of the day,
But left upon the bench no less
Than that day's gain in comeliness;
Then shut the door, and slowly went
Under the rose to bed, content.

    The man is dead, and leaves no name;
Thus softly from his workshop came
A thousand boxes, for the most
Broken, burnt, destroyed and lost.
This had its fellows once, but they
In all their beauty vanished away:
Some slip of fate let your box stay!

The Mistake

I HEARD a voice in midnight street,
  Someone crying softly below,
And pity sprang at the sound, to greet
  The grief of one I did not know.
All the city was quiet and deep;
  Only wind went through the limes.
'Grief must be bitter that cannot sleep,'
  I said; and heard the morning chimes,
And left my book, to lean above
  The empty street.   On lamplit leaves
I watched the sharp rays flash and move—
  'Who wakes,' I wondered, 'who is it grieves?'
Then plainly out of the shadows came
  The sister of that first sound of woe;
But now, the sound the very same,
  It was only a lover laughed below!

The Pearl in the Parable

LOVE is to some a duty
      Like rising to the sun,
And even so bound, is beauty . . .
      Or may be bought, or won,
Or may be suddenly captured,
      But even so caught still praised;
And passion, for the enraptured,
      Near love may tarry amazed.

But duty, conquest, purchase,
      And passion transfigured, wane
(Who once desiring searches
      May find and search again!):
Stars by the skies are proffered—
      Meadows their light flowers lift—
Life comes unasked, unoffered—
      Love at its strength is gift.

The White Fawn

BY downs we climbed above the earth;
    There, from a couch of thyme and turf,
We heard the wind go roaring by.
You spread your hands upon the grass,
      And in their span
Gentian bells and blue self-heal
And thyme among your fingers ran.

  Lift up your bright eyes again!
In that deep atlantic air
Between the lonely hills, or where,
Covered and drowned, the valley lies,
Sleeps the hollow of a land
Buried underneath the sea,
Where not long ago passed over,
      Happily as we,
Some barbarian and his golden lover,
Holding on leash between them then
      Time in rash captivity.

Deep and steep the cleavage went;
     And far and high
The line of hills rolled up, and spent
Their waves against the sky.

We stared forth at forests old,
Dark of gate at broadest noon,
That with their roots had taken hold
On slopes that should have cast them down,
So steep they were.   But still they clung,
Holding a hundred years of night
Defiantly against daylight,
Since youth, if they were ever young.

You spread your hands above the grass
Again, and in their little span
Lotus and potentilla flowered,
And thyme among your fingers ran.
What cloud, what question touched your mood,
        Evading thought?
Dark on its hill-top slept the wood,
        And still we heeded not.
When suddenly my wrist was caught—
We looked—and wonder made us dumb:
Up the valley, alone and afraid,
        We saw the white fawn come!

She seemed unreal, she was so small,
        Slender and white;
The one live creature lost in all
That hollow of wind and empty light.

And fear was in her swiftness, too:
We saw her run on delicate feet
Over the grass, and lift her head
To smell what danger she must meet
More than fear, from which, we knew,
      She timidly fled;
But while we watched, she climbed apace
To where dark woods do still begin,
And, looking upon their gloomy sides,
      Went easily in.

Cares Cast Away

CARES cast away like careful clothes, forgotten;
   Life's shivering hungry childhood out of doors—
Locked heartlessly outside; now, now Relentless,
The place, the time, the feckless persons yours.
Thrusting the world aside, future and past,
The wills of life and of us are one at last.

How bravely the pain of fire dissolves our bodies,
How worldless the air to which have climbed our wings;
Cruelty kisses love in our lips' encounters;
The last tendril of thought snaps and unclings.
Unpersoned we are; spilt from our crystal meekness;
Molten obedience now, neither strength nor weakness.

.   .   .   .   .

You have had your will, and we our wild overtaking.
Now at its best and worst let Time sweep by;
You will come again, to exact our pain and terror,
And pay yourself with the promise out of a cry;
You to whom pleasure and agony—both ours—
Are but the proof and profit of your powers.

Annunciation

SHE sees a far city
     Where Time never cumbers,
Where waver—the day long—
With soft noise at wall-side
Tall trees that lose never
One leaf to the by-race
Of clear-hearted water,
But for ever stand summer-bright
With birds in them bowered.

No highway, no gateway
Nor entry—yet arises
In fountains the acceptable
Sacrifice of laughter.
She hears.   And a moment
The daylight of delight
Flowers forth; and she wonders,
Calm before her fears.

To tell of this vision
Her maiden heart fails her;
She cannot, she cannot,
O terror that she cannot!
Altogether lonely,

By all laws bidden so,
Head bowed, hands folded,
Sure choosing she will enter;
Even for the terror
Of glory not falter,
Nor leave touch of finger-tip,
Nor glance, nor appealing
To us, her unhelpers
Beloved but fast bound.

Night Fear

THIS walled-in cube of candle-light
   Is all my world—the rest is night;
I know where stand, on every hand,
Gigantic tree-shapes out of sight;
I saw them fade when, shade by shade,
The night grew thicker in their land,
Till at a match my candle burned,
And windows into mirrors turned.

A moth can put this world to shame:
I live as lives my candle-flame;
These walls I see, which comfort me,
These windows where, as in a dream,
A shadow sits searching his wits,
Would all go out, and I should be
Disbodied, and my fear a spark
Of life upon the godless dark.
   In stillness, now, of other things,
   I hear the soft flutter of wings!

50215

Unknown Adam

A WEEK before you were born
The willows were ready,
And a high blue Easter sky
Had shut the winter away.

The time alone was our choice;
Whatéver you sháll be
Lies curled like a fern in your sleeping head,
Unknown Adam.

We called; but you fashioned yourself
To be this answer.
Nine months in secret you thought of yourself,
Fronded in mystery, hidden and heavy.
We named you in whispers.
At last, in an hour of terror we had our son.

The sharp air stings; the sun is brave;
The wind is eager; the little buds dance to it.
Early flowers hang over your cradle.
Your hands shut upon each other,
Your eyes open and we are strangers.

MADE AT THE

TEMPLE PRESS

LETCHWORTH

GREAT BRITAIN